I SPY
THANKSGIVING
BOOK FOR KIDS

This book belongs to

·····························

·····························

HAPPY THANKSGIVING

I SPY WITH MY LITTLE EYE SOMETHING STARTING WITH..

A

IS FOR

Apple pie

I SPY WITH MY LITTLE EYE SOMETHING STARTING WITH..

B
IS FOR
Bread

I SPY WITH MY LITTLE EYE SOMETHING STARTING WITH..

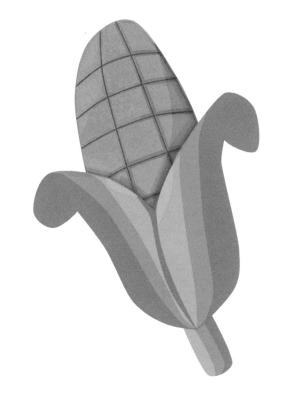

C
IS FOR
Corn

I SPY WITH MY LITTLE EYE SOMETHING STARTING WITH..

D
IS FOR

Dessert

I SPY WITH MY LITTLE EYE SOMETHING STARTING WITH..

E

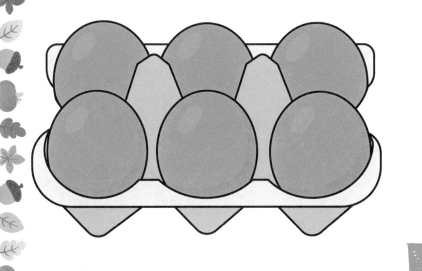

E

IS FOR

Eggs

I SPY WITH MY LITTLE EYE SOMETHING STARTING WITH..

G
IS FOR
Grapes

I SPY WITH MY LITTLE EYE SOMETHING STARTING WITH..

H
IS FOR

Hat

I SPY WITH MY LITTLE EYE SOMETHING STARTING WITH..

I
IS FOR

Ice cream

I SPY WITH MY LITTLE EYE SOMETHING STARTING WITH..

J

IS FOR

Jam

I SPY WITH MY LITTLE EYE SOMETHING STARTING WITH..

K
IS FOR
Kettle

I SPY WITH MY LITTLE EYE SOMETHING STARTING WITH..

L
IS FOR

Leaves

I SPY WITH MY LITTLE EYE SOMETHING STARTING WITH..

M
IS FOR
Meat

I SPY WITH MY LITTLE EYE SOMETHING STARTING WITH..

N

IS FOR

Native Americans

I SPY WITH MY LITTLE EYE SOMETHING STARTING WITH..

O

IS FOR

Owl

I SPY WITH MY LITTLE EYE SOMETHING STARTING WITH..

P
IS FOR
Pumpkin

I SPY WITH MY LITTLE EYE SOMETHING STARTING WITH..

Q

IS FOR

Queen

I SPY WITH MY LITTLE EYE SOMETHING STARTING WITH..

R
IS FOR
Rolls

I SPY WITH MY LITTLE EYE SOMETHING STARTING WITH..

IS FOR

Sauce

I SPY WITH MY LITTLE EYE SOMETHING STARTING WITH..

T
IS FOR

Turkey

I SPY WITH MY LITTLE EYE SOMETHING STARTING WITH..

U
IS FOR
Umbrella

I SPY WITH MY LITTLE EYE SOMETHING STARTING WITH..

V

IS FOR

Vegetables

I SPY WITH MY LITTLE EYE SOMETHING STARTING WITH..

W IS FOR

Wishbone

I SPY WITH MY LITTLE EYE SOMETHING STARTING WITH..

X

IS FOR

Xerus

I SPY WITH MY LITTLE EYE SOMETHING STARTING WITH..

Y IS FOR Yoyo

I SPY WITH MY LITTLE EYE SOMETHING STARTING WITH..

Z
IS FOR
Zucchini

FIND DIFFERENT PICTURE

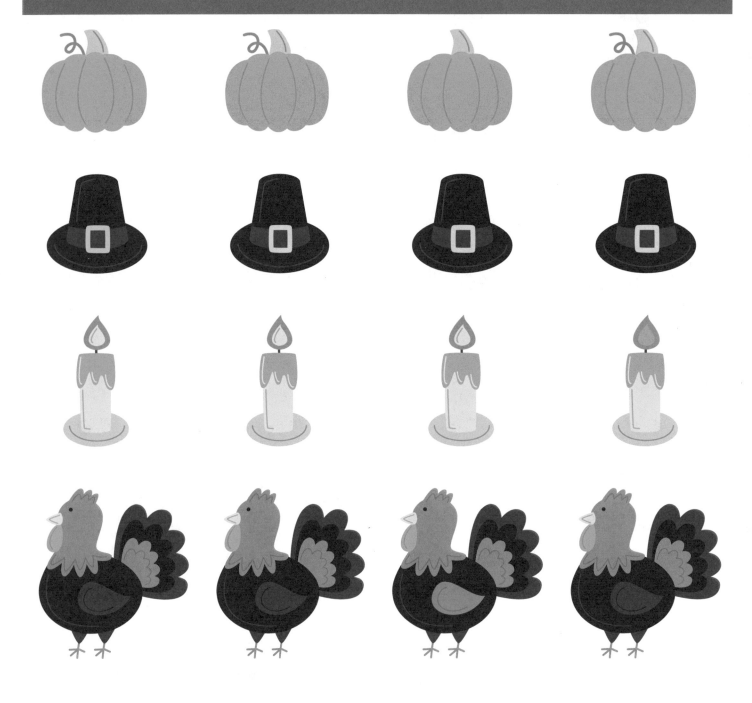

HOW MANY?

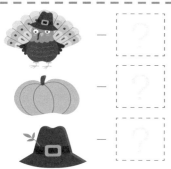 — ?

— ?

— ?

 — ?

— ?

— ?

 — ?

— ?

— ?

HANDWRITING PRACTICE

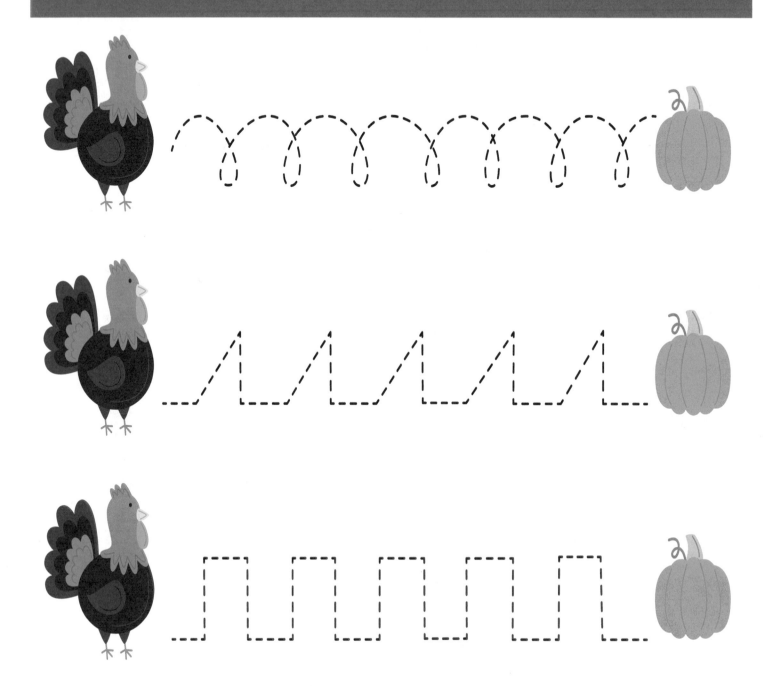

HANDWRITING PRACTICE

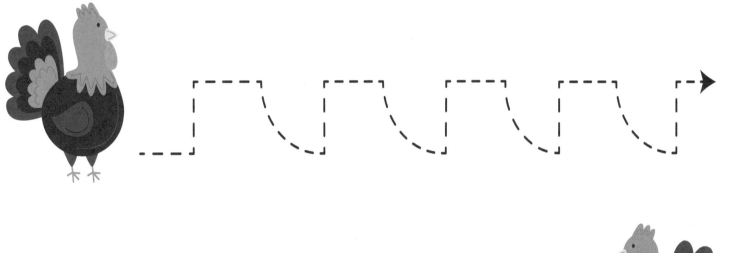

HANDWRITING PRACTICE

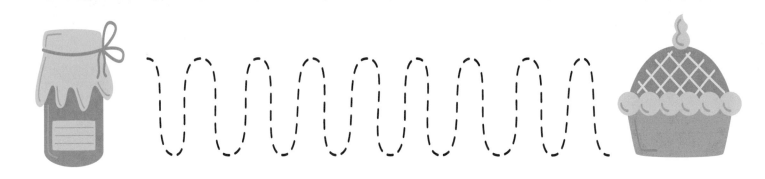

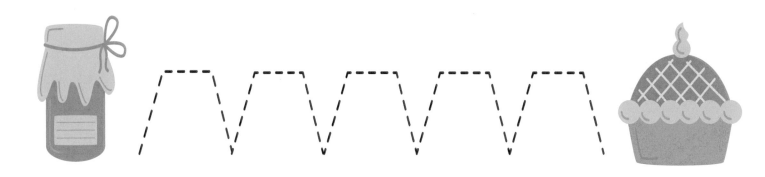

TRACE AND COLOR

TRACE AND COLOR

TRACE AND COLOR

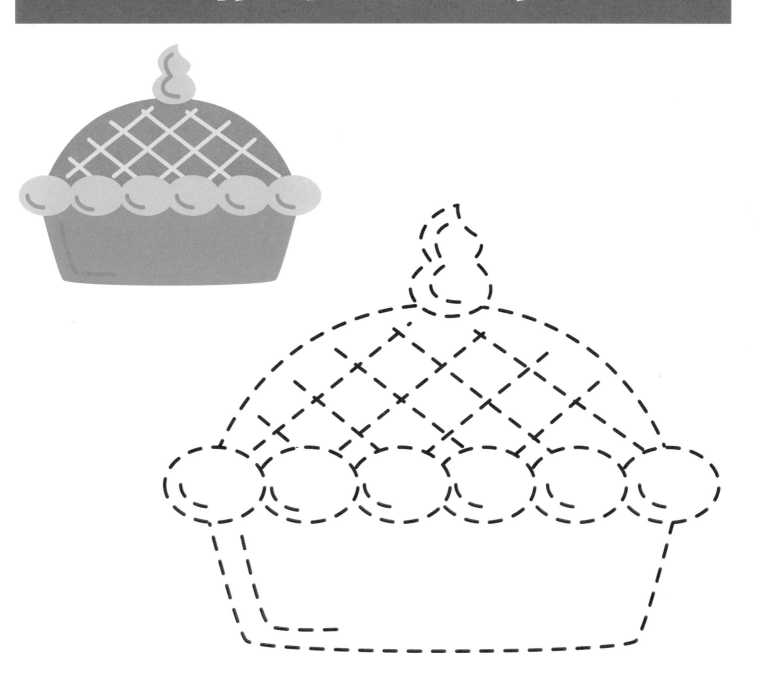

HOW MANY TO THE LEFT, HOW MANY TO THE RIGHT?

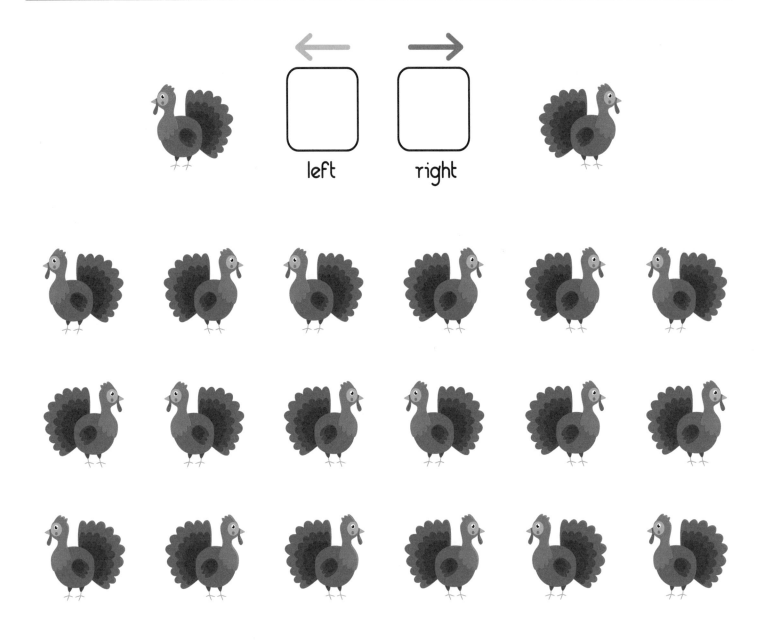

left   right

MORE, LESS OR EQUAL?

MATCH BY SIZE

FIND THE MISSING LETTER

_URKEY

T

D

F

FIND THE MISSING LETTER

X

W

H

_AT

FIND THE MISSING LETTER

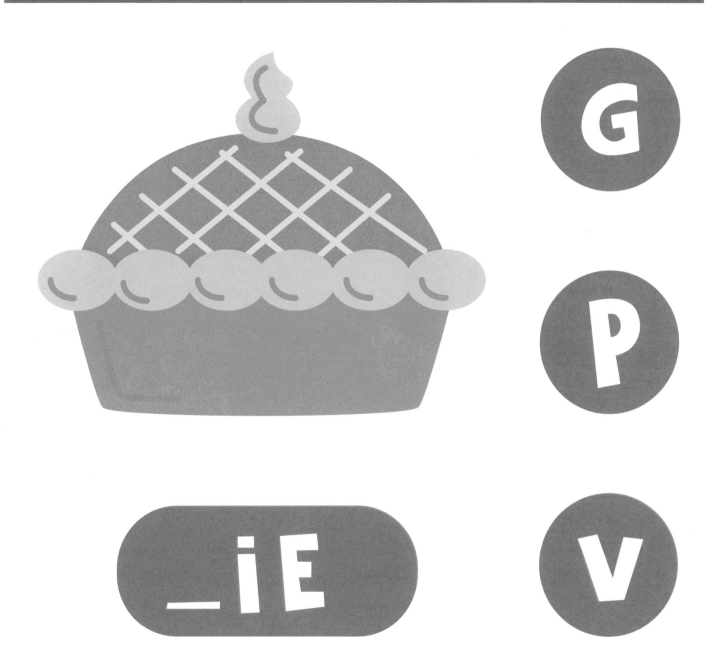

G

P

_IE

V

FIND 5 DIFFERENCES

GUESS THE WORD

K R U Y T E

COLOR BY NUMBERS

MAZE

Made in United States
Troutdale, OR
11/15/2024

24852280R00042